Published by Sourcebooks eXplore, an imprint of Sourcebooks Kids

P.O. Box 4410, Naperville, Illinois 60567–4410

(630) 961-3900

sourcebookskids.com

First published as Red Kangaroo's Thousands Physics Whys: *How to Make a Real Superhero: Radioactivity* in 2018 in China by China Children's Press and Publication Group.

Library of Congress Cataloging-in-Publication Data is on file with the publisher.

Source of Production: PrintPlus Limited, Shenzhen, Guangdong Province, China

Date of Production: August 2020

Run Number: 5018840

Printed and bound in China.

PP 10 9 8 7 6 5 4 3 2 1

Let's Get Glowing!

Revealing the Science of Radioactivity with Nuclear Physics

sourcebooks
eXplore

#1 Bestselling
Science Author for Kids
Chris Ferrie

Red Kangaroo sees a sign with the symbol she has seen in comic books. "Maybe this is the place where I can become a superhero with superpowers!" she says.

"This symbol is the sign for radiation. It is a warning," Dr. Chris says.

Red Kangaroo remembers being taught that radiation can be dangerous. "This means danger, right, Dr. Chris? Should we stay away from all radiation?"

"It is good to be careful and obey safety signs," Dr. Chris replies. "But everything in the world is radioactive! Some radioactive things occur naturally, like the **potassium** in a banana. Others are made to be radioactive, like a smoke detector using **americium**."

"Whoa! But these are safe, right Dr. Chris?" Red Kangaroo asks.

"Yes," Dr. Chris replies. "But I will tell you more about the physics of radioactivity so you understand. When you gain knowledge, then you are a real superhero!"

"Oops, you didn't need these, did you?" Red Kangaroo says.

"Everything is made of atoms. Every atom has a **nucleus** made of **protons** and **neutrons**," explains Dr. Chris.

"Oh, yes! Protons have a positive charge, which means they push away from each other, right?" asks Red Kangaroo.

"That's right!" Dr. Chris replies. "But in the small world of quantum physics, the nucleus wants to stay together."

"So the protons are confused," Red Kangaroo says.
"They can't decide what to do!"

"Sometimes the nucleus becomes unstable, and radiation shoots out!" Dr. Chris exclaims.

"Is it like a kettle used to boil water?" Red Kangaroo wonders. "When the water gets hotter and hotter, it explodes with steam."

"That's right!" says Dr. Chris. "When this happens with atoms, we call it **radioactive decay**."

"Hey, I recognize those as the first three letters of the Greek alphabet!" exclaims Red Kangaroo. "Scientists sure count in funny ways!"

"Alpha decay is when two protons and two neutrons shoot out of the nucleus together." explains Dr. Chris. "The bunch is called an alpha particle and it is really heavy! But that means it hits a lot of other things and stops very quickly. Even a thin piece of paper can stop alpha particles."

"Beta decay is what happens when a neutron turns into a proton," says Dr. Chris.

"But neutrons have no charge." Red Kangaroo repeats. "How can a neutron gain a positive charge?"

"Great question!" says Dr. Chris. "The total charge must stay the same, so that means beta decay shoots out an electron."

Dr. Chris

"It looks so fast!" exclaims Red Kangaroo.

"Yes!" Dr. Chris says. "It is moving close to the speed of light."

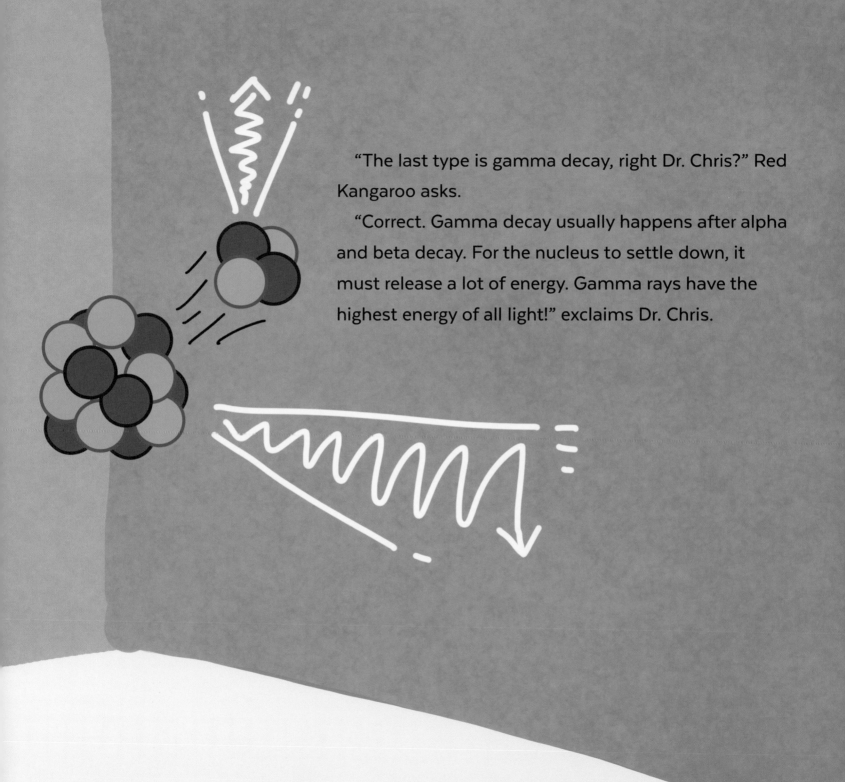

"The last type is gamma decay, right Dr. Chris?" Red Kangaroo asks.

"Correct. Gamma decay usually happens after alpha and beta decay. For the nucleus to settle down, it must release a lot of energy. Gamma rays have the highest energy of all light!" exclaims Dr. Chris.

"This all sounds scary!" worries Red Kangaroo. "Maybe we should just stay away from radioactivity!"

"Not so fast!" warns Dr. Chris. "Radioactivity can be dangerous, but safe radioactivity is everywhere! Many molecules in the air and soil are radioactive. Even your body is radioactive!"

"I've seen this machine in the hospital," says Red Kangaroo.

"This scanner uses radioactivity for medicine," says Dr. Chris. "It helps doctors see inside your body. When we harness the power of physics, anything is possible! But when we make powerful technology, we also need to be safe and protect those around us."

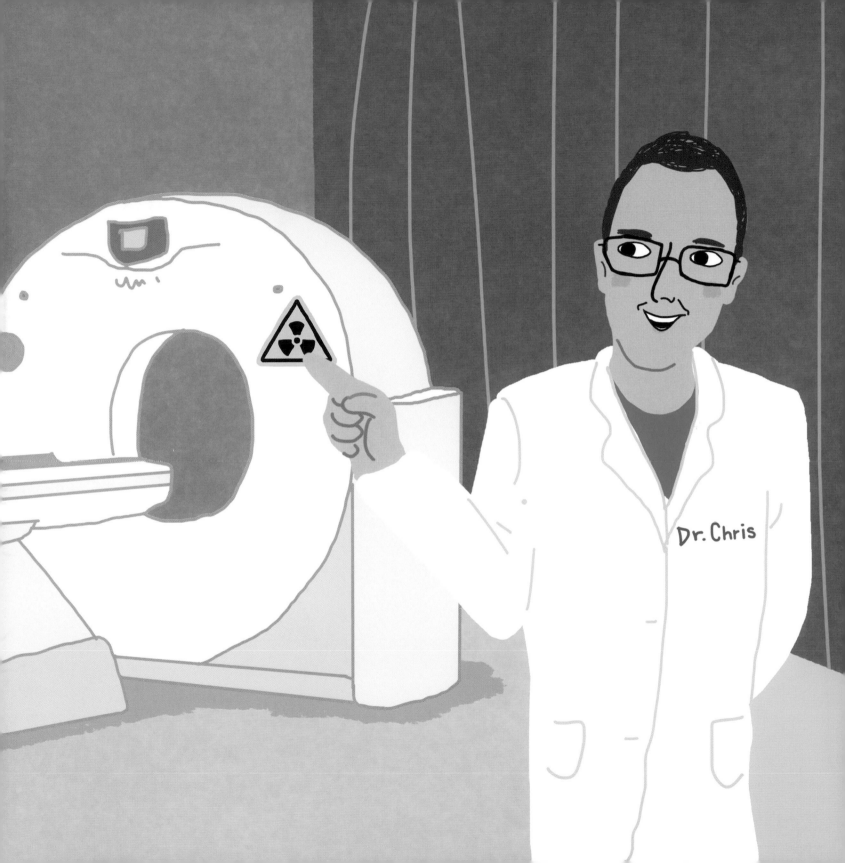

Now Red Kangaroo thinks differently about what it means to be a superhero. "If I am a very careful engineer or scientist, I can use radioactivity to make great discoveries and inventions!"

"I believe you can do it, Red Kangaroo!" says Dr. Chris.

Glossary

Americium
A human-made radioactive element used in smoke detectors.

Potassium
A naturally occurring radioactive element found in foods and in your body.

Nucleus
(*plural* nuclei). The center of an atom, which is made of densely packed neutrons and protons.

Radioactivity
When a nucleus is unstable and loses energy by emitting particles.

Radioactive Decay
The event of a radioactive element emitting an alpha, beta, or gamma particle.